Tanks

Henry Brook

Designed by Tom Lalonde and Zoe Wray

Illustrated by Adrian Roots, Paul Davidson and Giovanni Paulli

Edited by Alex Frith

Tank consultant: David Willey,
Curator of the Tank Museum, Bovington

Contents

What is a tank?

Tanks are war machines that have played a vital role in battles for almost 100 years. All tanks have extremely tough hulls to protect a crew, tracks to carry them across rough ground, and powerful guns to attack enemies.

Basic parts of a tank

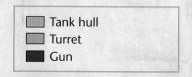

- Tank hull
- Turret
- Gun

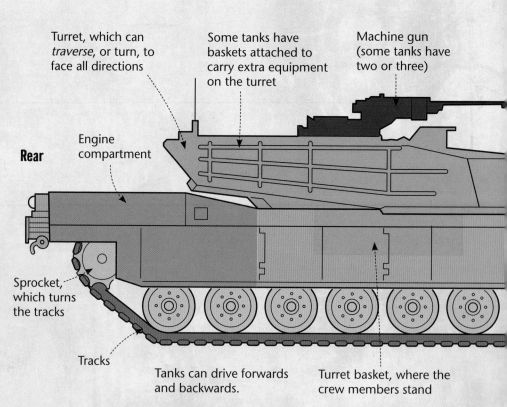

Turret, which can *traverse*, or turn, to face all directions

Some tanks have baskets attached to carry extra equipment on the turret

Machine gun (some tanks have two or three)

Rear

Engine compartment

Sprocket, which turns the tracks

Tracks

Tanks can drive forwards and backwards.

Turret basket, where the crew members stand

The crew

Tanks usually travel in groups of three or four,
known as a troop. Most tanks have a crew of four.

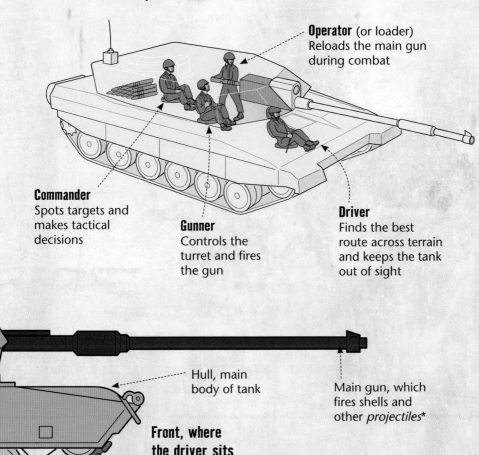

Operator (or loader)
Reloads the main gun
during combat

Commander
Spots targets and
makes tactical
decisions

Gunner
Controls the
turret and fires
the gun

Driver
Finds the best
route across terrain
and keeps the tank
out of sight

Hull, main
body of tank

Main gun, which
fires shells and
other *projectiles**

**Front, where
the driver sits**

Road wheels, which
support the tank

*Projectiles are missiles, or flying
weapons, fired out of a gun. Shells
contain explosives, but tanks also fire
projectiles that do not explode. Find
out more on pages 42-45.

Firepower

The most important feature of any tank is its main gun, mounted in the turret. It can fire a variety of missiles, designed to destroy enemy tanks and targets up to 5km (3 miles) away.

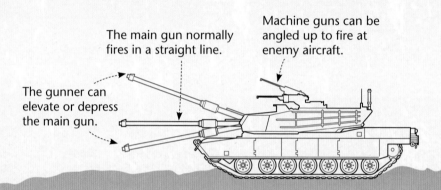

The main gun normally fires in a straight line.

Machine guns can be angled up to fire at enemy aircraft.

The gunner can elevate or depress the main gun.

Sensors help to aim the gun, and keep it steady. Find out more on pages 16-17.

Weapons on an M1 Abrams (1980–present)

❶ Main gun; barrel diameter 120mm

❷ Machine gun fired by operator

❸ Heavy machine gun fired by commander

❹ Operator crouching inside his hatch, or *cupola*

The M1 Abrams also has a grenade launcher and another machine gun next to the main gun.

This M1 Abrams has just fired. The flames are caused by the explosion that forces the missile out at incredibly high speed.

Keeping on track

All tanks run on tracks that give them incredible grip across all kinds of terrain.

This is an M1 Abrams driving through the desert in Iraq.

The tracks on this tank are covered with rubber pads to reduce wear and tear.

How to steer

Drivers use the tracks to steer. They can make one track turn faster than the other, and this pushes the tank around.

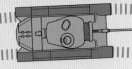

1. Both tracks turning at the same speed propels the tank forward

2. If the left track turns faster, the tank steers right

3. If the right track turns faster, the tank steers left.

Inside a Challenger 2

British Challenger 2 (1998–present)
- **Crew:** 4
- **Weapons:** 120mm main gun,
1 coaxial machine gun,
2 turret-mounted machine guns
- **Top speed:** 59km/h (37mph)

'Coaxial' means it always points the same way as the main gun. A tank's coaxial machine gun is usually next to the main gun.

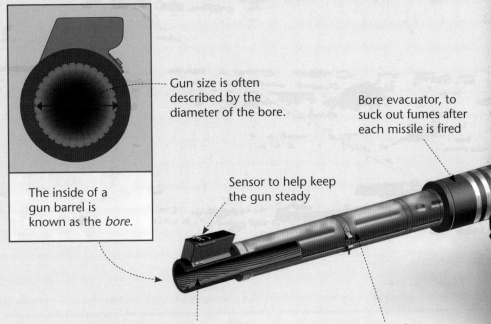

Gun size is often described by the diameter of the bore.

Bore evacuator, to suck out fumes after each missile is fired

The inside of a gun barrel is known as the *bore*.

Sensor to help keep the gun steady

British tanks have rifling in their main guns. Tanks from other countries often have unrifled, or 'smooth bore' guns. Smooth bore guns keep missiles accurate by firing them at very high speed.

The gun is wrapped in a thermal jacket, to keep it at a constant temperature.

Challenger 2

Challenger 2s are the toughest tanks
used by the British Army today.

Machine gun
connected to the
operator's cupola

Commander's cupola:
a hatchway where the
commander stands

Sights: behind each small
metal door is a set of
cameras to help the
commander and gunner
find targets by day or night.

Launchers
for smoke
grenades

Vision block:
window for the driver
to see through

Driver's hatchway

Safe ground

If tanks didn't have tracks, their wheels would press down in to the ground and easily get stuck. The track spreads the weight of the tank.

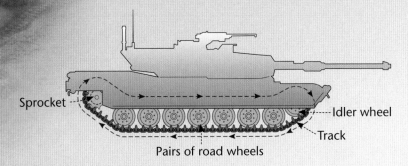

Sprocket

Idler wheel

Track

Pairs of road wheels

How tracks work

Teeth on the sprockets slot into links along the edge of the track. As the sprockets turn, they pull the track around.

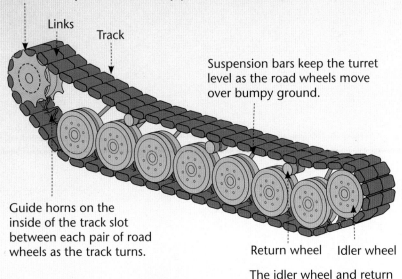

Links

Track

Suspension bars keep the turret level as the road wheels move over bumpy ground.

Guide horns on the inside of the track slot between each pair of road wheels as the track turns.

Return wheel   Idler wheel

The idler wheel and return wheels keep the track taut.

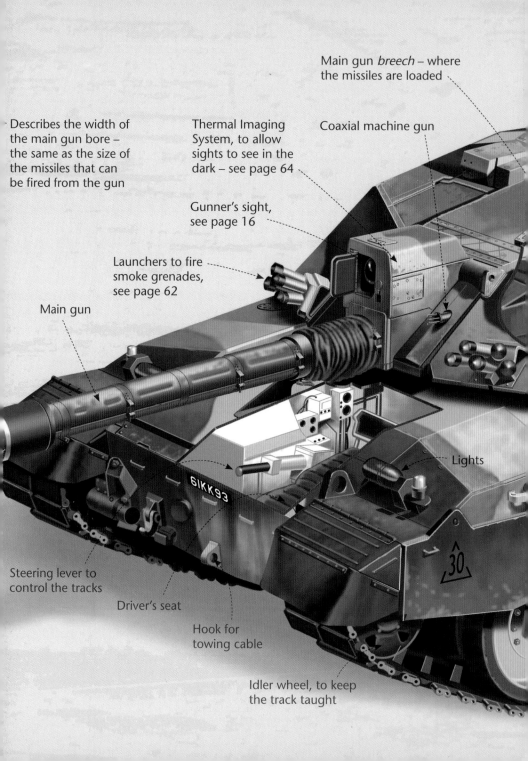

Main gun *breech* – where
the missiles are loaded

Describes the width of
the main gun bore –
the same as the size of
the missiles that can
be fired from the gun

Thermal Imaging
System, to allow
sights to see in the
dark – see page 64

Coaxial machine gun

Gunner's sight,
see page 16

Launchers to fire
smoke grenades,
see page 62

Main gun

Lights

6KK93

Steering lever to
control the tracks

Driver's seat

Hook for
towing cable

Idler wheel, to keep
the track taught

Sensors in this casing ensure the gun barrel stays straight to keep the gun on target.

Main gun

Grooves and ridges known as *rifling* line the inside of the gun barrel. These help missiles to fly more accurately.

Insignia to identify which part of the army the tank belongs to

Engine compartment, including the power pack, find out more on page 20

find out more on page 20

see page 8

Find out more on pages 42-45.

Tank weapons

- **Main gun:** fires missiles such as HEAT shells or Kinetic Energy penetrator projectiles. Find out more on pages 42-45.
- **Grenades:** Some tanks can also fire grenades – weapons that explode after a time delay.
- **Machine guns:** fire bullets to destroy enemy aircraft and infantry.

Drive sprocket, see page 8

The tank is painted with Disruptive Pattern Camouflage. This makes it harder to see the tank from far away, helping it hide from aircraft and satellite cameras.

Towing cable in case tank breaks down

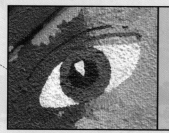

Many tanks crews give their tanks names, or paint mascots on the side. This tank has an eye to show it belongs to the 1st Royal Tank Regiment.

Commander's
sight, see page 16

Commander's
cupola

Communications mast

Ammunition racks,
where spare missiles for
the main gun are stored

Commander's
seat

Battle Management
System, find out
more on page 54

Road wheels

Steel tracks,
see page 8

Going for a drive

It's the driver's job to move the tank along. Skilled drivers pick out the best route across the terrain, trying to keep the tank out of sight.

The driver's compartment

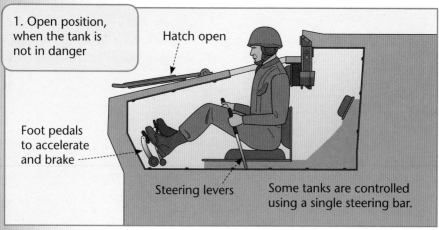

1. Open position, when the tank is not in danger

Hatch open

Foot pedals to accelerate and brake

Steering levers

Some tanks are controlled using a single steering bar.

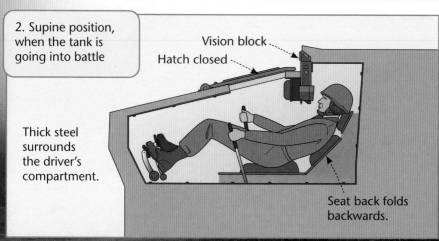

2. Supine position, when the tank is going into battle

Vision block

Hatch closed

Thick steel surrounds the driver's compartment.

Seat back folds backwards.

Training

Tank drivers learn using simulators. Each session can be recorded and played back, so the driver can see how well he has performed.

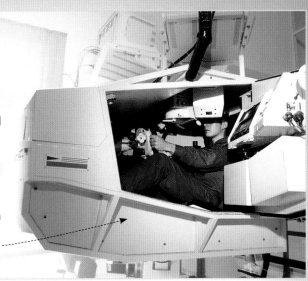

This driver is in a simulator for a Leclerc tank. -------

Most modern tanks have cameras on the rear of the hull, so the driver can see behind to reverse.

This British Challenger 2 is hiding in a 'hull down' position – the hull is hidden, but the gun turret has a clear line of sight.

Seeing out

Tank crews can ride with hatches open when the tank is not in danger. The commander, driver and operator each have a hatch.

The commander of a Challenger 2 stands in his cupola.

The crew use radio headsets to talk to each other.

Vision block

Vision block

Wiper to wash off mud and dust

Buttoned-up

In action, the crew 'button-up' – get inside and lock all hatches. They look out through camera sights, or small windows called vision blocks. The driver sits so low that his vision block works like a periscope.

Inside the driver's vision block

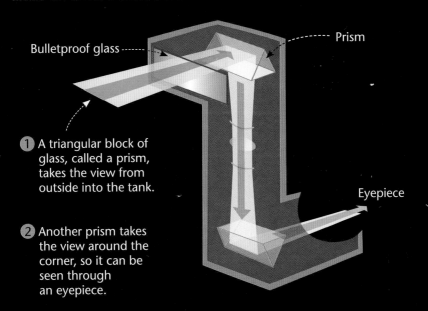

Bulletproof glass ------

------ Prism

1 A triangular block of glass, called a prism, takes the view from outside into the tank.

Eyepiece

2 Another prism takes the view around the corner, so it can be seen through an eyepiece.

View through the driver's vision block on a Challenger 2

Taking aim

In a Challenger 2, the commander and gunner both look for targets, using magnifying sights. Both can lock the sights onto a target.

This tank is visible in open countryside. In combat it would move quickly or hide to avoid being an easy target.

Fire Control

The gun is controlled by a network of computers known as a Fire Control System (FCS). Sensors around the gun and turret record wind speed and changes in air temperature. The computer uses this data to adjust the gun so it stays on target.

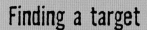

Finding a target

The commander can switch between day and night sights to pick out distant targets. Find out how night sights work on page 64.

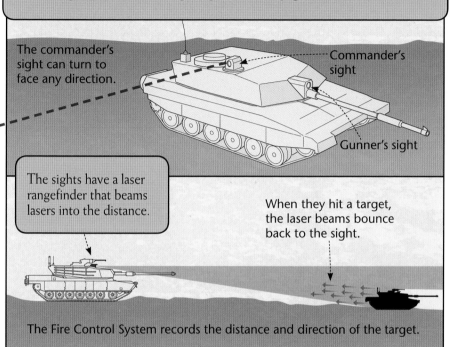

The commander's sight can turn to face any direction.

Commander's sight

Gunner's sight

The sights have a laser rangefinder that beams lasers into the distance.

When they hit a target, the laser beams bounce back to the sight.

The Fire Control System records the distance and direction of the target.

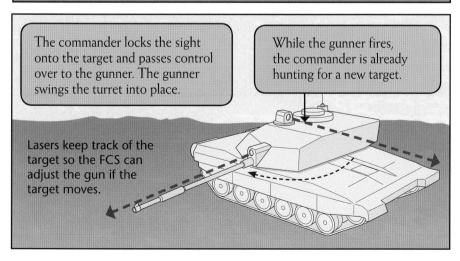

The commander locks the sight onto the target and passes control over to the gunner. The gunner swings the turret into place.

While the gunner fires, the commander is already hunting for a new target.

Lasers keep track of the target so the FCS can adjust the gun if the target moves.

Joystick controls

The commander and the gunner use joysticks to control their sights, the main gun, and the coaxial machine gun. Here's how the gunner's joystick looks on a Challenger 2:

A skilled tank crew can fire as many as eight missiles in under a minute.

Switches between day or thermal imaging night sights. See page 64.

Flips control from commander's joystick to gunner's joystick

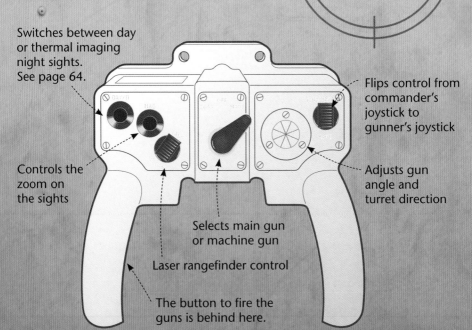

Controls the zoom on the sights

Adjusts gun angle and turret direction

Selects main gun or machine gun

Laser rangefinder control

The button to fire the guns is behind here.

Missile parts

This is a KE penetrator missile. Find out how it works on page 45.

The whole missile is about as big as a bodybuilder's arm.

Casing, which holds propellant to force the missile out at high speed

Warhead, which hits the target

Aim, load, fire!

First, the commander uses his sights to aim.

Commander

Gunner

He locks onto the target, and gives the order to fire.

Between shots, the operator grabs a new missile from the stockpile behind him...

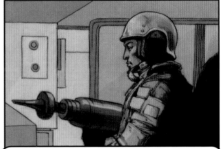

...and loads it into the breech. In some tanks, the operator adds a separate explosive charge behind each missile.

The gunner checks his sights are locked onto the target...

...and fires.

CLICK!

BOOOM!!!

Power pack

The biggest modern tanks need massive engines to propel them across rough terrain at speeds of up to 70km/h (45mph).

M1 Abrams tanks have a gas turbine engine. They're quieter than other tanks, but use up fuel more quickly.

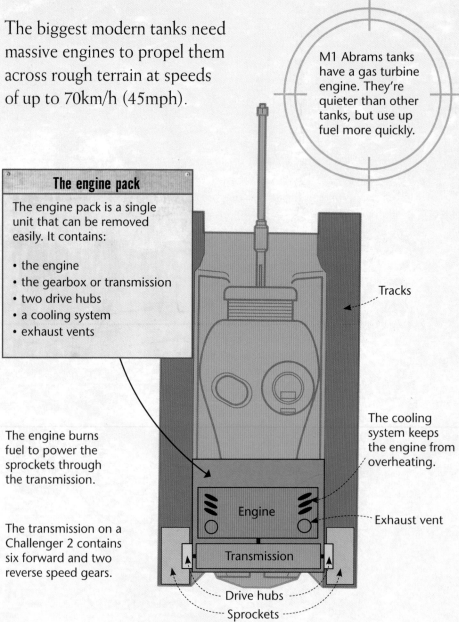

The engine pack

The engine pack is a single unit that can be removed easily. It contains:

- the engine
- the gearbox or transmission
- two drive hubs
- a cooling system
- exhaust vents

Tracks

The engine burns fuel to power the sprockets through the transmission.

The transmission on a Challenger 2 contains six forward and two reverse speed gears.

The cooling system keeps the engine from overheating.

Engine

Exhaust vent

Transmission

Drive hubs

Sprockets

Performance comparison chart			
	Max. speed	Fuel tank capacity	Max. distance on one tank of fuel
Challenger 2	59km/h (37mph)	1590 li (420 gallons)	450km (280 miles)
M1 Abrams	72km/h (45mph)	1900 li (500 gallons)	465km (290 miles)
Farm tractor	40km/h (25mph)	1325 li (350 gallons)	500km (310 miles)
4–wheel drive car	210km/h (130mph)	85 li (20 gallons)	915km (570 miles)

Breakdown recovery

Tank crews used to make repairs on the battlefield. Modern crews simply wait for engineers from a support vehicle to replace the entire engine pack.

Army engineers replacing the engine pack on a Merkava. The whole operation can be completed in 15 minutes.

The first tank

Tanks were invented by the British Army nearly a hundred years ago, to cross the churned-up battlefields of the First World War (1914-1918).

British Mark I tanks first stormed into combat in 1916.

British Army officials watch a prototype Mark I tank moving across a muddy park.

The crew lifted steel flaps to look out.

The Mark I had no turret. It had two main guns in cabins on either side of the hull.

The front line of battle during the War was marked with trenches – open tunnels where soldiers lived. Mark I tanks were designed to cross a standard 3m (9ft) wide trench.

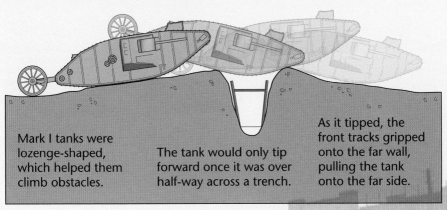

Mark I tanks were lozenge-shaped, which helped them climb obstacles.

The tank would only tip forward once it was over half-way across a trench.

As it tipped, the front tracks gripped onto the far wall, pulling the tank onto the far side.

Mark Is had a steel hull that could stop bullets, but they weren't tough enough to stop missile shells.

British Mark I (1915–1918)

- **Crew:** 8
- **Firepower:** 2 main guns, 4 machine guns
- **Max. hull thickness:** 12mm (0.5in)
- **Top speed:** 6km/h (4mph)

The Mark I in action

On September 15, 1916, the British sent their new weapon – the Mark I tank – rumbling towards enemy trenches in northern France. British generals were hoping the tanks would smash through the German line, and end the months-long Battle of the Somme.

German soldiers ran in horror, as dozens of tanks crashed through their heavily fortified trench system.

Most bullets couldn't pierce the tank's hull, but the impact knocked shards of hot metal off the insides.

This picture shows chain mail masks that later tank crews wore for protection.

Within a few hours, the Mark Is had captured several villages deep in enemy territory.

With no radios or phones, some crews used pigeons to send urgent messages to their commanders.

But the attack was badly planned. Many tanks broke down or got stuck in shell holes and wide trenches. The battle dragged on until November, ending in a stalemate.

Tanks take over

By the end of the First World War, Britain had improved upon the Mark I. Other countries developed their own tanks, too.

This two-man tank had the first fully traversing tank turret.

French Char Renault FT–17 light tank (1917–1945)

- **Crew:** 2
- **Firepower:** 37mm main gun or 1 machine gun
- **Max. hull thickness:** 22mm (0.8in)
- **Top speed:** 7km/h (4mph)

For a long time, tanks were divided into three categories – *light*, *medium* and *heavy* – depending on their size and the job they were designed to do.

British Mark A medium tank 'The Whippet' (1918–1930)

- **Crew:** 3
- **Firepower:** 4 machine guns
- **Max. hull thickness:** 14mm (0.6in)
- **Top speed:** 13km/h (8mph)

The Whippet was speedy for a tank, even across rough ground. It had two engines – one for each track.

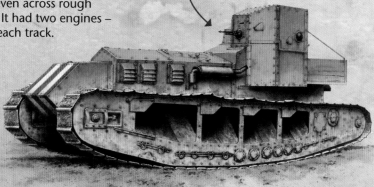

British Mark IV (1917–1918)

- **Crew:** 8
- **Firepower:** 2 57mm main guns, 4 machine guns
- **Max. hull thickness:** 12mm (0.5in)
- **Top speed:** 8km/h (5mph)

Over a thousand Mark IVs reached the battlefields of the First World War.

German tanks were known as *panzers*. The A7V was Germany's first panzer, but this massive machine was top-heavy and only drove well on roads.

German A7V panzer (1918)

- **Crew:** 18
- **Firepower:** 57mm large main gun, 6 machine guns
- **Max. hull thickness:** 30mm (1.2in)
- **Top speed:** 15km/h (9mph)

British soldiers relax next to a re-captured Mark IV, and a newly captured German A7V.

Giants collide

In April 1918, three Mark IVs were on patrol outside the village of Villers-Bretonneux in northern France, when three German A7V monster tanks approached from the village of Cachy.

The air was so hot and full of smoke in early tanks, crews often passed out.

The world's first tank versus tank battle began...

Both tanks have German black crosses painted on them.

The Battle of Villers-Bretonneux

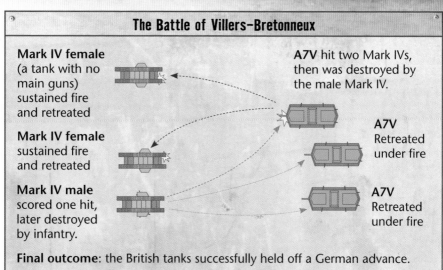

Mark IV female (a tank with no main guns) sustained fire and retreated

Mark IV female sustained fire and retreated

Mark IV male scored one hit, later destroyed by infantry.

A7V hit two Mark IVs, then was destroyed by the male Mark IV.

A7V Retreated under fire

A7V Retreated under fire

Final outcome: the British tanks successfully held off a German advance.

antry tanks were
igned to advance
oss the roughest
und, supporting
antry attacks.

duced
re than the
anzers.

**British A22 Mk IV infantry tank
'Churchill'** (1941–1952)

- **Crew:** 5
- **Firepower:** 57mm main gun
- **Max. hull thickness:** 102mm (4in)
- **Top speed:** 25km/h (15.5mph)

**Russian T-34/76A
medium tank** (1940–1958)

- **rew:** 4
- **irepower:** 76.2mm main gun,
  machine guns
- **ax. hull thickness:** 65mm (2.6in)
- **op speed:** 40km/h (25mph)

The T-34 had wide tracks,
sloping hull shape and a
hard-punching gun. It was a
very successful tank.

Allied tanks

The two sides in the war were known as the Allies and the Axis powers. On the Allied side were Britain, the Soviet Union, the USA and other allies.

Inf
de
ac
gr
inf

American M4 medium tank 'Sherman' (1942-1955)

- **Crew:** 5
- **Firepower:** 76mm main gun, and 2 or 3 machine guns
- **Max. hull thickness:** 75mm (3in)
- **Top speed:** 48km/h (30mph)

American factory workers pr
almost 50,000 Shermans, mo
total number of all German ρ

British A12 MkII infantry tank 'Matilda II' (1939-1945)

- **Crew:** 4
- **Firepower:** 40mm main gun and 2 machine guns
- **Max. hull thickness:** 78mm (3.1in)
- **Top speed:** 13km/h (8mph)

Known as the 'Queen of the Desert' to British soldiers in North Africa, the Matilda II had a thick hull making it very hard to destroy.

The Second World War

During the Second World War (1939-1945), the tank emerged as the dominant land weapon.

At first, the Germans used light, fast tanks to penetrate deep into enemy positions. But, as the fighting went on, both sides used stronger, heavier tanks with big guns to try to rule the battlefields.

Russian T-34 tanks roll into battle alongside ground troops in 1943.

Panzer is short for PanzerKampfwagen, the proper German word for tank.

German panzer III medium tank (1939-1945)

- **Crew:** 5
- **Firepower:** 50mm main gun, 2 or 3 machine guns
- **Max. hull thickness:** 50mm (2in)
- **Top speed:** 40km/h (25mph)

The most successful panzer commanders became celebrities in Germany.

'Carro Pesante'
k (1943-1945)

m main gun,

ss: 50mm (2in)
/h (26mph)

r V medium tank
' (1943-1945)

m main gun,

ss: 120mm (4.7in)
/h (28.5mph)

German panzer VI heavy tank 'Tiger 1' (1942-1945)

- **Crew:** 5
- **Firepower:** 88mm main gun, 2 or 3 machine guns
- **Max. hull thickness:** 100mm (4in)
- **Top speed:** 37km/h (23mph)

Axis tanks

The Axis powers were made up of Germany,
Italy and their allies, and later Japan.

In the early days of the Second World War, the Panzer III was
used to smash through enemy forces, cutting their supply
lines to the battlefield and causing mayhem.

Weak, unreliable and badly equipped, the
Italian tanks were no match for the British
forces in the North African desert.

Italian P26/4 heavy ta

- **Crew:** 4
- **Firepower:** 75m
  1 machine gun
- **Max. hull thickn**
- **Top speed:** 42kr

German panz 'Panthe

- **Crew:** 5
- **Firepower:** 75m
  1 machine gur
- **Max. hull thickn**
- **Top speed:** 46kr

Speedy, hard to knock out and
armed with a deadly accurate gun,
over 6,000 Panthers were made.

Panzer bashers

When German forces invaded the Soviet Union in 1941, they ran into a secret weapon: the T-34. Easy to build and hard to knock out, it could outpace and outfight panzers. It was probably the best tank of the war.

This 1943 T-34 had a massive 85mm main gun, the most powerful gun at the time.

The all-round, sloping hull deflected missiles and was copied by the Germans for the Panther.

Other Russian giants

KV-1 heavy tank

The KV-1 boasted a hull so thick German troops had to use an anti-aircraft gun to penetrate it.

JS-3 heavy tank

Nicknamed 'the Frying Pan', because of the shape of its turret

The T-34 was a no-nonsense fighting machine, put together without any thought for crew comfort or good looks.

Its low height made the tank difficult to spot and hit.

Broad tracks ploughed through muddy ground at high speed.

The engine ran on diesel fuel, much safer than old gasoline engines.

King of the road

One of the most feared tanks of the war was the German Panzer VI – the Tiger. It carried a whopping 88mm gun, and its hull was so thick Allied crews saw their missiles bounce off, even at close range.

Hunting Tigers

Tiger crews shuddered in fear the first time Allied planes swooped down and shot at them...

A Tiger rolls through a Sicilian village in 1943.

...only to find that the bullets bounced off the thick hulls.

For Tiger and all tank crews a new danger appeared with an anti-tank weapon known as a HEAT missile. Find out more on page 42.

Spare tracks attached to the hull provided extra protection from shells.

The King Tiger

The Tiger II, or King Tiger, was a monster tank, armed with an upgraded, longer 88mm gun.

But it was made in too few numbers and came too late to save Germany's war effort.

Tiger on the rampage

German Commander Michael Wittmann and his Tiger crew had been fighting in Russia for three years. But in June 1944 they were sent as part of the German effort to stop the Allied invasion of France, known as the D-Day landings.

On the morning of June 13, outside the town of Villers-Bocage, a column of British tanks was advancing. Little did they know that a troop of enemy tanks was watching them, among them Wittmann's Tiger...

Wittmann led the attack, blasting at the line of British vehicles.

He charged into Villers-Bocage leaving a trail of burning tanks and wounded soldiers behind his Tiger.

Wittmann's rampage finally ended when an anti-tank gun smashed the Tiger's drive sprocket, locking the tracks, but he escaped with his crew. The lone Tiger had destroyed over 20 British vehicles.

A winning workhorse

The American M4 tank, or 'Sherman', was a support tank for infantry attacks. It wasn't especially tough, and didn't have a massive gun, but lots could be made very quickly.

Sherman Firefly

Many British troops also used American-built Shermans. Most troops of four included one adapted Sherman known as the Firefly.

High-velocity 76mm gun

These tanks had a huge main gun, strong enough to destroy a German Tiger.

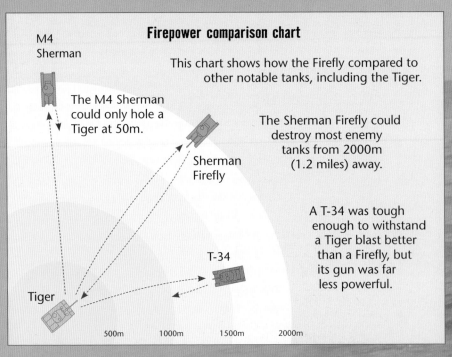

Firepower comparison chart

M4 Sherman

This chart shows how the Firefly compared to other notable tanks, including the Tiger.

The M4 Sherman could only hole a Tiger at 50m.

Sherman Firefly

The Sherman Firefly could destroy most enemy tanks from 2000m (1.2 miles) away.

A T-34 was tough enough to withstand a Tiger blast better than a Firefly, but its gun was far less powerful.

T-34

Tiger

500m 1000m 1500m 2000m

US tanks are often named after generals. Sherman was a successful general of the American Civil War.

A Sherman tank rolls off a transport ship onto a beach in a trial run for the D-Day landings.

The funnies

To help the Allies fight their way into France on D-Day – June 6, 1944 – many Shermans were converted in unusual ways. These tanks were known as the *funnies*.

Sherman Crab

Long chains attached to a spinning drum helped clear away mines on beaches.

Churchill Crocodile

As well as the main gun, the Crocodile also had a flame-thrower.

Burst of flame from the flamethower

Fuel for the flame-thrower was stored in a trailer.

Sherman Duplex Drive

Duplex Drive, or 'DD', tanks could roll off boats while still at sea, then *swim* to shore from as far as 11km (7 miles), ready to blow up machine-gun posts and concrete bunkers.

A screen was raised around the tank to keep it afloat.

The screen was kept up by pumping hoses with air

Two propellers drove the tank through the water. This was known as a 'Duplex Drive' system.

A Sherman DD drives off a landing craft into the sea.

Anti-tank weapons

Early in the Second World War, soldiers began using High Explosive Anti-Tank missiles, also known as HEAT missiles. This new weapon could pierce even the thickest hulls.

Ground troops launch a Javelin – a modern guided HEAT missile.

Types of HEAT missiles		Fired from:
• **Projectile** – travels as far as the gun launches it.		Tank guns
• **Rocket/Grenade** – carries a motor to propel it after it's fired.		Rocket launchers
• **Guided missile** – carries a motor for extra propulsion, and a guidance system to help it find the target.		Rocket launchers; tank guns

Long range

Warhead

By 1942, infantry used hand-held launchers, often known as *bazookas*, to fire HEAT missiles at tanks from a distance of 90m (100 yards) away.

The latest HEAT missiles, such as the Javelin, contain two HEAT charges in their warheads to break through the toughest modern tank hulls.

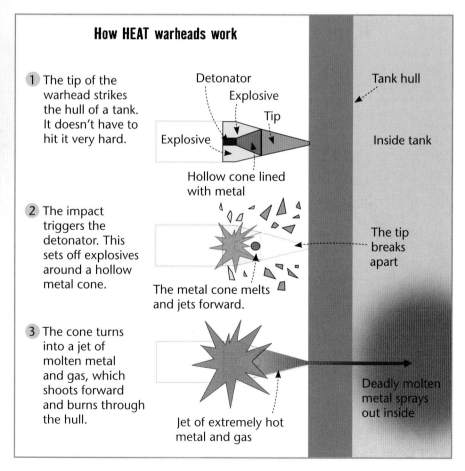

How HEAT warheads work

1. The tip of the warhead strikes the hull of a tank. It doesn't have to hit it very hard.

   Detonator
   Explosive
   Tip
   Explosive
   Hollow cone lined with metal
   Tank hull
   Inside tank

2. The impact triggers the detonator. This sets off explosives around a hollow metal cone.

   The metal cone melts and jets forward.
   The tip breaks apart

3. The cone turns into a jet of molten metal and gas, which shoots forward and burns through the hull.

   Jet of extremely hot metal and gas
   Deadly molten metal sprays out inside

Some brave soldiers destroyed tanks by fixing explosive mines directly to the hulls.

One accurate hit from a HEAT missile can be enough to knock out even the best tanks.

This German *Sturmgeschutz*, or assault gun, had a thicker hull than most panzers but was easily destroyed by an anti-tank missile.

Penetrators

The Kinetic Energy (KE) penetrator, or Fin round, is even more deadly than a HEAT missile. It's a long metal arrow that pierces a tank's hull through sheer momentum.

This is the part of the projectile that flies out of the main gun.

Each holds a long, slim arrow of super-dense metal.

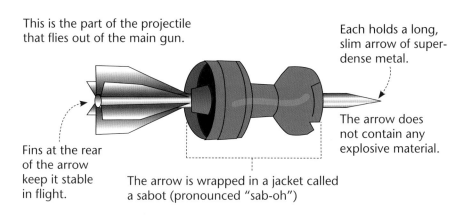

Fins at the rear of the arrow keep it stable in flight.

The arrow does not contain any explosive material.

The arrow is wrapped in a jacket called a sabot (pronounced "sab-oh")

How KE penetrators work

1. The fire button activates explosives in the tank's main gun, shooting the arrow out at high speed.

2. After the shell leaves the barrel, the sabot breaks and falls off.

3. The force of the arrow is concentrated onto a tiny area on the target.

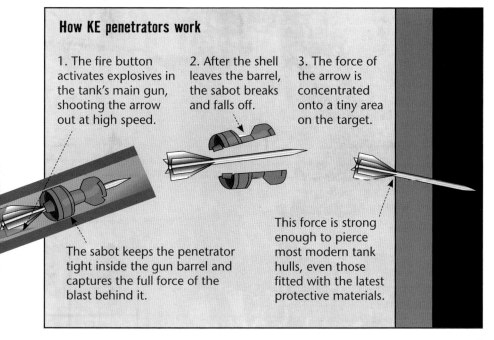

The sabot keeps the penetrator tight inside the gun barrel and captures the full force of the blast behind it.

This force is strong enough to pierce most modern tank hulls, even those fitted with the latest protective materials.

The Cold War

The Second World War was followed by a 40-year struggle known as the Cold War. Hostility brewed between countries in eastern Europe, led by the Soviet Union, and the West, led by the USA. Both sides built vast quantities of new tanks.

The Russian army's T-54, and its later variant, the T-55, are the most widely produced tanks in history. Over 50,000 were built, and many T-55s are still in use today.

Russian T-54 (1950–present)

- **Crew:** 4
- **Firepower:** 100mm main gun; 3 machine guns
- **Max. hull thickness:** 200mm (8in)
- **Top speed:** 55 km/h (34mph)

American M60 (1961–1997)

- **Crew:** 4
- **Firepower:** 105mm main gun; 2 machine guns
- **Max. hull thickness:** 150mm (6in)
- **Top speed:** 48km/h (30mph)

The M60 was based on an earlier design of tank known as the 'Patton', and is sometimes referred to as a Patton tank.

The name Patton comes from General Patton, one of the most famous tank generals of the Second World War.

German Leopard I (1965-2003)

- **Crew:** 4
- **Firepower:** 105mm main gun, 2 machine guns
- **Max. hull thickness:** 70mm (3in)
- **Top speed:** 65km/h (40mph)

The Leopard I was fast across all kinds of terrain, and had a devastatingly powerful main gun.

British Chieftain (1966-1995)

- **Crew:** 4
- **Firepower:** 120mm main gun, 2 machine guns
- **Max. hull thickness:** 195mm (7in)
- **Top speed:** 48km/h (30mph)

The Chieftain was the first tank to let the driver lie in the flat, or supine, position. This meant the whole tank could be lower to the ground, and so easier to hide.

Main battle tanks

Designers stopped building light, medium and heavy tanks and tried to combine the strengths of all three in one machine. These multi-task fighting vehicles are called *main battle tanks*.

High-tech tanks

Low, sleek and packed with new technology, the Russian
T-72 was so impressive that western armies set to work
designing their own high-tech tanks to compete with it.

A snorkel allowed the crew of
the T-72 to breathe when the
tank crossed deep rivers.

The tank's turret was
incredibly low to the
ground, helping it hide.

Russian T-72 (1971–present)

- **Crew:** 3
- **Firepower:** 125mm main gun;
  2 machine guns
- **Top speed:** 80km/h (50mph)

The turret was so low the crew had
to be shorter than most soldiers.

The T-72 had a machine called an
autoloader to load the main gun, so
it only needed a crew of three.

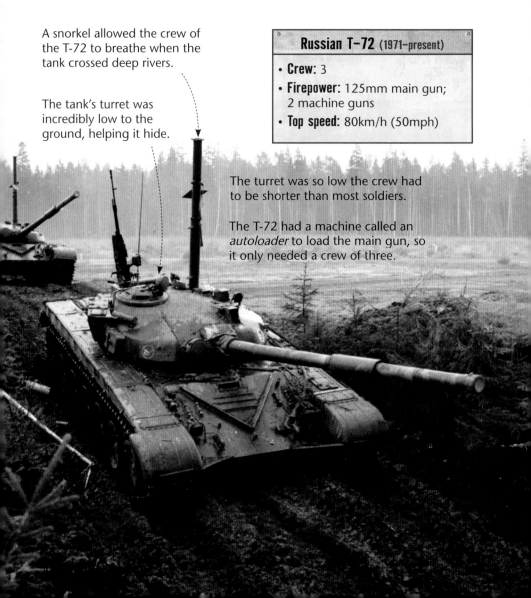

Better protection

One key feature of modern British and American tanks was a new kind of protection, known as Chobham. This was a *composite* – made of layers of different materials – that helped lessen the impact of all kinds of missiles.

American M1 Abrams (1980–present)

- **Crew:** 4
- **Firepower:** 105mm main gun; 2 machine guns
- **Top speed:** 72km/h (45mph)

With its revolutionary gas-turbine (jet) engine, the M1 Abrams had astonishing speed and mobility.

British Challenger 1 (1983–1990s)

- **Crew:** 4
- **Firepower:** 120mm main gun, 2 machine guns
- **Top speed:** 60km/h (37mph)

The first Abrams and Challenger tanks were both built with Chobham hulls. The exact design of Chobham remains top secret.

A deadly accurate main gun made the Challenger I a world-class main battle tank.

A Challenger 1 once destroyed an enemy Iraqi tank over 5km (3 miles) away – the furthest recorded hit from a tank.

Desert Storm

In February 1991, Russian-built tanks faced US tanks in combat. The fighting took place in the desert nation of Kuwait.

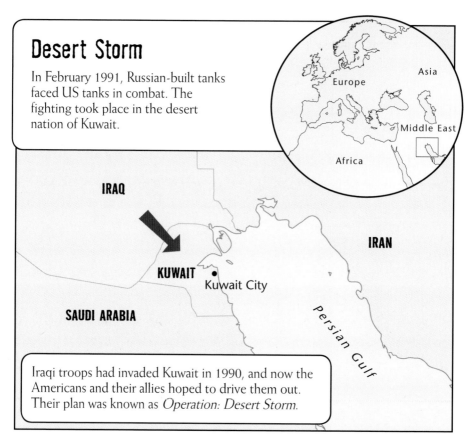

Europe

Asia

Middle East

Africa

IRAQ

IRAN

KUWAIT

Kuwait City

SAUDI ARABIA

Persian Gulf

Iraqi troops had invaded Kuwait in 1990, and now the Americans and their allies hoped to drive them out. Their plan was known as *Operation: Desert Storm.*

Iraqi troops were equipped with Russian-built T-72s.

The US sent hundreds of M1 Abrams tanks into Kuwait by ship and plane.

Phase 1: The US airforce launched air strikes against the Iraqi troops.

Phase 2: US tank crews, aided by British crews in Challenger 1s, drove into the attack under dust clouds.

They used state-of-the-art night vision sights to find and target enemy tanks.

The T-72s had caused a stir in the 1970s, but in 1991 they were no match for the well-trained crews of the Abrams and Challengers. Just 100 hours after the operation began, Kuwait was liberated, and a ceasefire was called.

Tanks today

Here are some of the most powerful tanks in use today. Most have hulls made of composite materials such as Chobham.

The T-90 is fitted with laser units that can confuse enemy detection equipment. Find out more on page 63.

Russian T-90 (1994–present)

- **Crew:** 3
- **Firepower:** 125mm main gun; 2 machine guns
- **Top speed:** 60km/h (37mph)

German Leopard II (1979–present)

- **Crew:** 4
- **Firepower:** 120mm main gun; 2 machine guns
- **Top speed:** 72km/h (45mph)

The Leopard II can fully traverse its turret in just 7 seconds – faster than any other tank.

French Leclerc
(1990–present)

- **Crew:** 3
- **Firepower:** 120mm main gun, 2 machine guns
- **Top speed:** 72km/h (45mph)

The Leclerc is one of the lightest and fastest tanks in the world.

American Abrams M1A2
(1996–present)

- **Crew:** 4
- **Firepower:** 120mm cannon, 3 machine guns
- **Top speed:** 67km/h (42mph)

The M1A2 Abrams was the first tank to have separate sights for the commander and gunner that could both lock onto targets.

Israeli Merkava Mk1 (1979–present)

- **Crew:** 4
- **Firepower:** 105mm cannon; 3 machine guns
- **Top speed:** 46km/h (30mph)

The Merkava has its engine mounted at the front of the driving compartment, as an extra barrier against enemy shells.

On the battlefield

Tank commanders can view and share live battle information with Army Headquarters (HQ) and other combat units, through a computer-based Battle Management System.

The red arrows show how information is passed around.

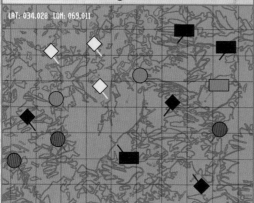

Battle Management Screen

LAT: 034.028 LON: 069.011

HQ

Soldiers at HQ use images from satellites and planes to keep the map of battle up to date.

Information is organized at HQ and sent to a screen in each tank turret, to show tank commanders the location of friendly forces and enemy targets.

Support vehicles travel with the tanks. Find out more on page 70.

Ground troops

What are our orders?

Ground troops stay in touch with HQ and tank commanders via a secure radio network.

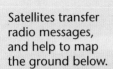

Satellites transfer radio messages, and help to map the ground below.

Aerial photo showing a military complex

Unmanned spotter planes take photos to help map the ongoing battle. This photo shows mountainous terrain in Iraq.

Spotter plane

Bomber planes

Troop commanders can call bomber planes to provide air support.

Tank troop

Enemy tanks

Tank commander

The enemy is in sight.

Commanders can update HQ's Battle Management System with new information, based on what they see through the tank sights.

Protection

This Challenger 2 is fitted with the latest protective measures.

Modern tanks carry a dazzling range of defensive systems to keep crews safe on the battlefield.

Coated glass on the vision blocks protects the crew's eyes from laser attacks.

Heat-reflecting panels identify it as a "friendly" to gunners in the same type of tank.

Some tanks carry anti-missile systems that can intercept missiles and blow them up before they hit the tank.

Camouflage nets are kept rolled up to be deployed quickly – see page 58.

Extra steel plates, or reactive plates (see right), can be bolted on for further protection.

Filters and piping channel heat away from the back of the tank to confuse heat-seeking missiles.

Spare missiles are stored in containers surrounded by liquid, to reduce the chance of a fire if the tank is hit.

How reactive plating works

Some kinds of reactive plating have a layer of explosive sandwiched between layers of metal.

Explosive ----->

Metal ----->

Hull ----->

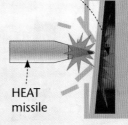

When a missile hits, it ignites the explosive.

HEAT missile

The metal breaks apart and flies away from the tank, deflecting the jet of hot metal from the missile.

Explosive reactive plating isn't always used because the flying metal can hit friendly infantry.

Watertight

Most tanks have a watertight hull and can cross rivers up to 1.5m (5ft) deep. Some can even go completely underwater.

The crew of this Leopard II have attached a snorkel to the commander's cupola. The whole tank can now travel in water up to 4m (13ft) deep.

Airtight

Tanks aren't entirely airtight, but they use two methods to keep the air in the turret clean and safe.

☐ **Pressurized cabins**

The air inside the turret is kept at a higher pressure than air outside. This keeps outside air from getting in.

● **Air filters**

Filters in the hull can absorb harmful gases and trap hazardous particles.

Most modern tanks are designed to be safe from four major types of hazards – known as CBRN:

Chemical   Biological   Radiological   Nuclear

The commander uses his headset to give instructions to the driver.

Cables support the snorkel as it pushes through the water.

Snorkel

A cap is placed on the gun to stop water getting into the barrel.

Crossing deep rivers saves time and fuel in battle if a bridge has been blown up.

Camouflage

Tanks use different types of camouflage to make them harder to spot.

Camouflage screens – netting made of fabric – break up the outline of the tank, helping it to blend in with the background.

This Leopard II is covered with a set of screens to help it hide in the desert.

Modern camouflage netting is designed to hide moving tanks from aircraft and satellite cameras.

Camouflage can't completely hide a vehicle – but it makes it harder for the enemy to work out exactly what it is, and which weapons to fire at it.

Living under cover

When a tank is parked, or *leagured*, crews use branches as well as netting to hide it.

The crew have to cook, eat, sleep and even go to the toilet under the nets, too.

Some screens can absorb heat and reflect light, hiding the tank from night sights and laser rangefinders.

The barrel of the gun on a Merkava pokes out through a smokescreen.

Smoke clouds

Tanks can produce thick clouds of smoke to hide in before charging into battle.

1. The tank fires a volley of smoke grenades up into the air.

2. The grenades explode in mid air, sending out a wide umbrella of smoke.

3. The smoke falls to the ground making a thick cloud. It covers an area of 38m (100ft) in diameter, lasting for about 4 minutes.

Smokescreen

Tanks can also produce a continuous stream of smoke behind them, by dripping fuel into their exhaust vents. This is often used when retreating under fire.

Lightscreen

Some Russian tanks are fitted with a protection system known as Shtora. This hides the tank from cameras, lasers and computer sensors.

A T-90 fitted with a Shtora system drives across a shallow river.

Shtora protective system

- Shtora can detect lasers from enemy rangefinders, and even work out where they came from.

- It can spray gas which makes the tank invisible to night vision cameras.

- Two *dazzler units* use secret technology to raise a curtain of heat energy around the tank that confuses many anti-tank weapons.

Dazzler units

Night fighting

To see in dark and difficult conditions, the gunner uses his TOGS – Thermal Observatory and Gunnery Sight.

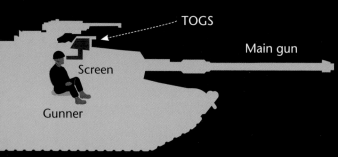

TOGS

Main gun

Screen

Gunner

TOGS on a Challenger 2

Thermal detector picks up heat given off by vehicles and soldiers.

TOGS also include *light intensifiers*. These detect low-level lighting so the soldiers can see things invisible to the naked eye.

Light intensifiers create a digital image on a screen in green. Human eyes can detect more varieties of green than any other shade.

View through the TOGS of an M1 Abrams in Baghdad, Iraq at night, showing friendly tanks.

Scaling down

Tanks are very expensive to build and run, and hard to move far because of their weight. Designers are working to perfect smaller, more versatile fighting vehicles.

American M2 Bradley Infantry Fighting Vehicle (IFV)
(1981–present)

- **Capacity:** 2 crew + 6 soldiers
- **Firepower:** Small main gun or machine gun
- **Top speed:** 66km/h (41mph)

The Bradley and the Stryker are used for peacekeeping and to carry troops. They don't have the thick hulls and heavy firepower of a main battle tank.

Canadian/American Stryker IFV
(2002–present)

- **Capacity:** 2 crew + 9 soldiers
- **Firepower:** 1 large main gun, 6 machine guns
- **Top speed:** 100km/h (62mph)

There are more than 11 variants of the Stryker, used for all sorts of jobs from carrying big guns to providing medical support.

Drone tanks

Some new fighting vehicles are unmanned robot tanks known as drones. These might one day be used to carry out tasks in dangerous combat zones.

British Black Knight Unmanned Combat Vehicle
(2010–present)

- **Crew:** 0
- **Firepower:** 30mm main gun, 1 machine gun
- **Top speed:** 77km/h (48mph)

Black Knight can be used like other tanks but is operated by remote control.

American Gladiator Tactical Unmanned Ground Vehicle
(2007–present)

- **Crew:** 0
- **Firepower:** 1 machine gun
- **Top speed:** 24km/h (15mph)

Gladiator is a scouting vehicle, used to take pictures. But it also carries a machine gun.

Drone tanks in action

In the future, most tanks could be unmanned drones. Here's how they might be used:

In a distant war zone, soldiers in trouble call for help.

Within minutes, a transport plane drops a light drone tank near the battle.

Thousands of miles away, a driver in a simulator starts up the tank using radio signals.

Satellites photograph and map the war zone, sending the information to the soldier in the simulator.

Watching live camera pictures from the tank, the driver takes the drone into battle.

Sharing the load

Tanks rely on other tracked vehicles to clear battlefield obstacles and support them with fuel and spare parts.

British Trojan AVRE (2008–present)

- **Type:** Combat Engineer Vehicle
- **Based on:** Challenger 2 tank
- **Use:** to clear mines and other obstacles so tanks can pass into combat zones

Excavator arm ┄┄┄┄

Rolls of plastic pipes that can be laid over trenches or muddy ┄┄┄┄ ground to allow tanks to cross

Bridgelayers carry metal sections that unfold to become bridges.

American M60A1 AVLB (1960–present)

- **Type:** Bridgelayer
- **Based on:** M60 tank
- **Use:** to carry and lay down a bridge to help tanks cross over gaps of up to 18m (59ft)

This crane can lower a spare power pack into a Challenger.

Engineer vehicles like the Trojan often carry a machine gun for protection, but they aren't used as combat vehicles.

British Chieftain Mark 7 ARRV (1960s–1990s)

- **Type:** Repair and Recovery Vehicle
- **Based on:** Chieftain tank
- **Use:** to repair and recover broken down tanks and other vehicles

Bulldozer blade to dig up and safely detonate mines

The very first tanks

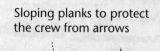

Sloping planks to protect the crew from arrows

Wooden tank (Italy, around 1485)

Italian artist and inventor Leonardo Da Vinci designed a fully-enclosed wooden tank, but he didn't build it.

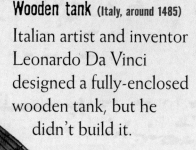

A full-size working replica stands in the Da Vinci Museum in Florence, Italy.

Simms' Motor War Car (UK, 1902)

The Motor War Car was one of the first engine-powered vehicles adapted for war. But it could only drive on roads, and was never used in combat.

It carried three guns.

Steel hull ----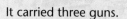

Little Willie (UK, 1915)

Little Willie was the nickname for the first successful tank prototype developed by the British Army. It helped engineers design the Mark I tank.

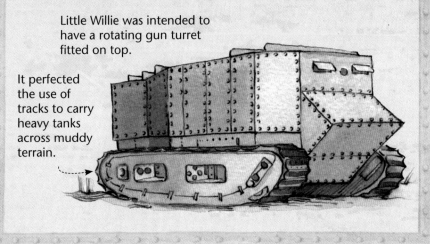

Little Willie was intended to have a rotating gun turret fitted on top.

It perfected the use of tracks to carry heavy tanks across muddy terrain.

Where did the name tank come from?

The original tanks were developed in secret by the British Army. The earliest, Little Willie, looked a little like a big water tank.

If the enemy saw the vehicle, and heard it called a tank, they might think it just held water. The name 'tank' stuck.

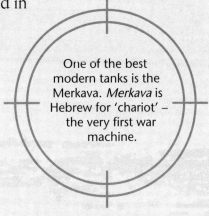

One of the best modern tanks is the Merkava. *Merkava* is Hebrew for 'chariot' – the very first war machine.

Tanks on the internet

There are lots of websites with information about tanks old and new. At the Usborne Quicklinks Website, you'll find links to some great sites where you can:

- Watch video clips of tanks in training
- Find out where you can go to explore inside a tank
- See a list of tanks used in the Second World War
- Read about the exploits of famous tank commanders

An M1 Abrams fires a missile.

When using the internet please follow the internet safety guidelines displayed on the Usborne Quicklinks Website. The recommended websites in Usborne Quicklinks are regularly reviewed and updated, but Usborne Publishing Ltd. is not responsible for the content or availability of any website other than its own. We recommend that children are supervized while using the internet.

For links to websites all about tanks, go to the Usborne Quicklinks Website at **www.usborne-quicklinks.com** and enter the keyword **tanks**.

Glossary

This glossary explains some of the words used in this book. If a word is written in *italic* type, it has an entry of its own.

ammunition A store of bullets or *missiles*.

anti-tank weapon A *missile*, bullet or grenade designed to destroy *tanks*.

autoloader A machine that selects and loads *missiles* into the *main gun*.

basket A steel drum that hangs and turns inside the *turret*. The turret crew sit in this basket.

bore evacuator A hollow drum around the *main gun* barrel which draws smoke and other gases away from the *turret*.

camouflage Methods used to hide or disguise a tank, such as paint or netting.

Chobham Top secret *composite* material used on modern *hulls*, developed by British scientists.

coaxial machine gun A *machine gun* attached to the *turret* that points in the same direction as the *main gun*.

commander The leader of a *tank* crew. The commander is responsible for the overall fighting efficiency of the *tank*.

composite Made up of many layers of different materials.

cupola A low, protective screen around the *commander's hatch*.

drive sprocket A toothed wheel powered by the engine that turns a *tank's tracks*.

Fire Control System The sensors, computer and *laser rangefinder* that help a *tank's main gun* to fire accurately.

friendly Tanks, troops or other vehicles fighting on the same side are friendly.

gas turbine engine A propulsion unit that burns fuel to turn fan blades and produce mechanical power.

gunner *Tank* crew member who controls and fires the *main gun*.

hatch The opening and door into a *tank hull* or *turret*.

HEAT An *anti-tank weapon*. HEAT stands for High-Explosive Anti-Tank.

hull The main body of a *tank* between the *tracks* and the *turret*.

idler wheel A wheel that keeps the *track* tight and stops it coming off.

infantry Soldiers who fight on the ground.

KE missile A *projectile* that uses high speed and momentum to smash through a target. KE stands for kinetic energy.

laser A beam of light that can strike a target and be used to accurately measure the distance to that target.

laser rangefinder A computer-controlled sensor that measures the distance from a *tank* to a target using *lasers*.

machine gun A gun that fires bullets rapidly.

main gun A gun that fires missiles, found on the *turret* of a *tank*.

mine An explosive device hidden in the ground, designed to blow up when a *tank* rolls over it.

missile A flying weapon such as a *shell* or a *rocket*.

night vision Equipment that boosts available light, and measures heat differences between objects, to help crews see in dark or dusty conditions.

loader *See operator.*

operator The crew member who loads the *main gun* and carries out other tasks to help the *commander*. Also known as the *loader*.

panzer Short for *panzerkampfwagen*, the German word for *tank*.

penetrator *See KE missile.*

persicope A tube that uses mirrors to provide outside views from within a *tank*.

power pack A single unit that contains a *tank's* engine and *transmission*.

projectile A *missile* fired by a gun that has no means of self-propulsion, unlike a *rocket*.

range The distance between a gun or other weapon and its target.

rifling A spiral of grooves and ridges insides a gun barrel that makes a missile spin as it accelerates, to improve accuracy.

road wheel A wheel that helps to support the weight of a *tank*.

rocket A *missile* that has an engine to help it fly.

sabot A cover around a *KE missile* to keep it tight inside a gun barrel. Pronounced "sab-oh".

shell A *projectile* that contains explosive.

smooth bore A gun barrel with no *rifling*, which can fire missiles very fast.

supine The lying-down position for a *tank* driver.

suspension Equipment that absorbs bumps and shocks from the *track* and *road wheels* to give a *tank* a smooth ride

tank A heavily-protected combat vehicle that runs on *tracks* and has firepower.

tracks Links of steel plates that form a continuous loop on either side of the *tank*. Tracks spread the weight of a *tank* and give it strong grip on loose or muddy ground.

transmission The connection between the engine and the *drive sprocket* that turns the *tracks*.

traverse To turn the *turret* and *main gun*.

turret The top part of a tank that holds the *main gun*. The *commander*, *gunner* and *operator* sit in the turret.

vision block — a small, bullet-proof window in the *tank*, often linked to a *periscope*.

Index

Page numbers marked with an 'a' are found underneath the flap on that page.

Acknowledgements

Every effort has been made to trace and acknowledge ownership of copyright. If any rights have been omitted, the publishers offer to rectify this in any future editions following notification. The publishers are grateful to the following individuals and organizations for permission to reproduce material on the following pages: (t=top, b=bottom, r=right, l=left)

cover Sherman tank © Corbis; **p1** Soviet tanks, Russia, 1943 © Art media/Photolibrary.uk.com; **p7** © Photo courtesy of Defenseimagery.mil and Sgt. Alex C. Sauceda, U.S. Marine Corps.; **p8-9** © General Dynamics Land Systems; **p13** (t) © Frederic Pitchal/Sygma/Corbis; **p14** © Mirrorpix/Getty Images; **p21** © Petr Josek/ X00396/Reuters/Corbis; **p22-23** Topical Press Agency/Getty Images; **p26-27** all © Osprey Publishing: (tl) Peter Sarson, *The Renault FT Light Tank* (bl) Mike Fuller, *88 mm FlaK 18/36/37/41 and PaK 43 1936–45*; (tr) Tony Bryan, *British Mark IV Tank* (br) Brian Delf, *German Panzer 1914-18*; **p28-29** © The Tank Museum, Bovington; **p30-31** © Sovfoto; **p30a** all © Osprey Publishing: (tr) Mike Chappell & Peter Sarson, *Churchill 1941-51*, (tl) Howard Gerrard & Jim Laurier, *Panther vs Sherman*, (br) Various Artists, *Panther vs T-34*, (tl) Peter Sarson, *Matilda Infantry Tank 1938-45*; **p31a** (tl) © ArtTech/Aerospace Publishing, the rest all © Osprey Publishing: (tr) Ian Palmer & Giuseppe Rava, *M3 Medium Tank vs Panzer III*, (bl) Howard Gerrard & Jim Laurier, *Panther vs Sherman*, (br) Various Artists, *Sherman Firefly vs Tiger*; **p32-33** © Sovfoto; **p33** KV-1 Peter Sarson, *KV-1 & 2 Heavy Tanks 1939–45* © Osprey Publishing, JS-3 © ArtTech/Aerospace Publishing; **p34-35** © ullsteinbild/TopFoto; **p35** Peter Sarson, *KingTiger Heavy Tank 1942-45* © Osprey Publishing; **p38** Various Artists, *Sherman Firefly vs Tiger* © Osprey Publishing; **p39** © Bettmann/Corbis; S. Navy photo by Chief Yeoman Alphonso Braggs; **p40** both © Osprey Publishing: Tony Bryan, *Sherman Crab Flail Tank*, Tony Bryan, *Churchill Crocodile Flamethrower*; **p42-43** U.S. Army photo by Gary L. Kieffer; **p44** © Popperfoto/ Getty Images; **p46-47** all © Osprey Publishing: (tl) Hugh Johnson, *T-54 and T-55 Main Battle Tanks 1944- 2004*, (bl) Jim Laurier, *M60 Main Battle Tank 1960-91*, (tr) Peter Sarson, *Leopard 1 Main Battle Tank 1965-95*, (br) Peter Sarson, *Chieftain Main Battle Tank 1965-2003*; **p48** © ITAR-TASS/Sovfoto, **p49** both © Osprey Publishing: (t) Peter Sarson, *M1 Abrams Main Battle Tank 1982-92*, (b) Peter Sarson, *Challenger Main Battle Tank 1982-97*; **p55** © Geoeye/Science Photo Library; **p56-57** © Tony Nicoletti/epa/Corbis; **p58-59** © Maurizio Gambarini/Picture Alliance/Photoshot; **p62** © Mohammed Saber/epa/Corbis; **p63** © Zastol`skiy Victor Leonidovich / Shutterstock; **p64-65** Photo courtesy of Defenseimagery.mil and Staff Sgt. Shane A. Cuomo, U.S. Air Force; **p70-71** © Colin C. Hill / Alamy; **p70** (b) Jim Laurier, *M60 Main Battle Tank 1960–91* © Osprey Publishing; **p71** (t) Peter Sarson, *Chieftain Main Battle Tank 1965–2003* © Osprey Publishing; **p74-75** Photo courtesy of Defenseimagery.mil and Cpl. Jason D. Mills, U.S. Marine Corps. Use of photos from Defenseimagery.mil does not imply or constitute U.S. Department of Defense endorsement.

With thanks to Osprey Publishing, www.ospreypublishing.com and to Cpt. Matthew Leary and the 1st Royal Tank Regiment at Warminster. Photos of the Challenger 2 supplied by Henry Brook, Tom Lalonde and Brian Voakes.

Additional illustrations by Ian McNee, Zoe Wray and Tom Lalonde
Additional designs by Jessica Johnson and Samantha Barrett   Digital design by John Russell
Series editor: Jane Chisholm   Series designer: Zoe Wray
Picture research by Ruth King   Additional editorial material by Lisa Gillespie